HYBRID PICK
COUNTRY AND MOD
GUITAR STYLES

by Wyn Pearson

Video
dv.melbay.com/21343
You Tube
www.melbay.com/21343V

Online Video

Video Contents

MEL BAY®

1 2 3 4 5 6 7 8 9 0

Visit us on the Web at www.melbay.com — E-mail us at email@melbay.com

contents

INTRODUCTION

Hybrid Picking is a combination of two techniques; fingerstyle and pick.

This technique is not common to any one particular genre. Once mastered, Hybrid Picking will bring fluidity to your playing, regardless of the style of music.

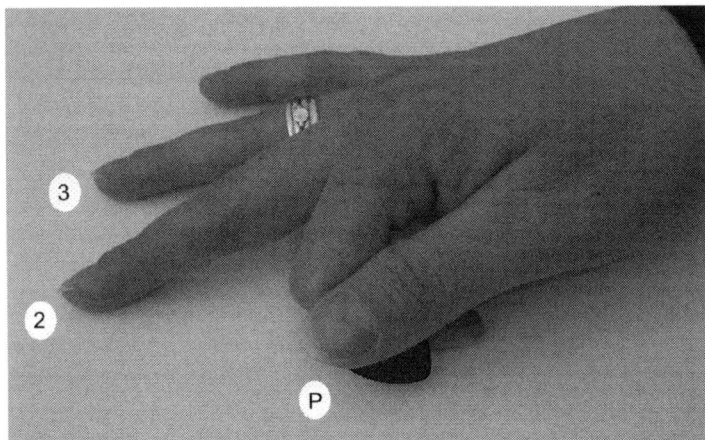

The pick is held between the thumb and index finger, which allows for standard pick technique, while the middle (2) and ring (3) fingers work independently. Players that are completely new to Hybrid Picking will find this to be the first real challenge.

The right hand must find a place to rest on the guitar body, usually on top of the bridge. This may need to change slightly, depending on the guitar used.

Be careful not to have any unnecessary muting of the strings, particularly the lower ones. The right hand should be completely relaxed with no tension in the second and third fingers.

Getting Started

DVD VIDEO   Track 1

Example 1

This first exercise can be used as an ideal way of strengthening the first and second fingers.
Try and produce each note with a separate movement rather than simply rolling the whole hand across the strings. Keep the wrist as still as possible.

♩ = 120

Example 2

For this example, although the pattern is the same, the pace is doubled.

♩ = 120

Example 3

It is very important to be rhythmically accurate with this next example, because we are simply repeating a three note pattern. It shouldn't be too difficult to play this at tempo after a little practice.

♩ = 120

Example 4

Here we have an example with a distinct country feel. Unlike the previous three exercises, this riff does not rely on a constant repeating pattern of notes. This makes it considerably more difficult to play. It does however help to enable independent articulation of the fingers.

♩ = 120

Example 5

This "banjo—like" final example relies heavily on rhythmical accuracy and good right-hand technique. The first measure introduces a fourth string for the first time. If Hybrid Picking is a totally new technique, the third finger will be harder to control than the second. Take care not to strike the first and second strings accidentally at the same time. The second measure is merely a three note repeated pattern made more difficult by a syncopated rhythm. Measure three is fairly straightforward and includes a hammer—on. The fourth measure like the first uses four strings. The rate of change for the third finger is now a little quicker. Example 5 sounds very effective at both slow and fast tempos.

CHAPTER 2

Leaping across 3, 4 and 5 strings

DVD VIDEO | Track 2

In this chapter we will look at ways in which Hybrid Picking can be used as a means of making three, four and five string leaps easier to play than using just the pick. These kinds of riffs can quite often have more fluidity by employing the hybrid technique, as pick technique alone can sometimes slow phrases down, particularly when leaping across strings.

Example 1

Example 1 is a straightforward blues scale phrase made more interesting by the inclusion of the leap from the D# to the top A and back again. The left-hand first finger should be placed across strings one and two at the start of the example.

Example 2

Example 2 is very similar to Example 1. This time however the phrase starts with a bend rather than a slide. Note also the two palm muted notes near the end, which have been added to give a more punchy effect to the riff (this technique is a precursor to "Chicken Pickin", Chapter 6). If you have strictly adhered to the right hand stance described in the Introduction, this palm muting should be relatively straightforward. Make the most of the accented notes at the end of the phrase.

Example 3

Example 3 is a combination of the ideas employed in the previous two examples. The first leap is exactly the same as before, but this time the phrase has been extended to a second measure, which includes a five string leap. The tempo has been increased a little.

Example 4

This next example is primarily based on a Pentatonic scale and includes another five string leap.
It is useful to place the first finger of the left hand across the third, fourth and fifth strings for beats one and two, then move to strings one and two for the remainder of the measure.

Example 5

Example 5 is a question and answer phrase, using a combination of techniques. String bending, slides, muting and string leaps all come together to make up a considerably challenging exercise.

Example 6

Example 6 uses open string bounce–downs, a technique that is synonymous with country music which works particularly well in the key of G Major. This riff sounds a lot more difficult to play than the required left-hand fingering would suggest.

Example 7

The 16th note passage at the end of the first measure of Example 7 would be extremely difficult to play at tempo using the pick alone. Try and keep the first finger of the left hand on the tenth fret, covering strings one and two for the first measure.

Example 8

The final example in this chapter requires particular attention to right-hand fingering. It is tempting to push the tempo when practicing a riff such as this, so using a metronome is advisable. The opening six notes can be difficult to execute well because of the third finger. Note that the opening has similar fingering to that of Example 4 in Chapter 1.

Arpeggios

DVD VIDEO · Track 3

Arpeggios are the notes of a chord played in succession rather than simultaneously. When used in context, these "broken" chords are a very effective way of adding flair to lead playing. The examples in this chapter should prove to be fairly straightforward, once the initial technique has been mastered. Attention to right hand detail is important from the start.

Example 1

Example 1 is made up of notes of a second inversion A major triad. The first finger of the left hand should be held across strings one and two. As far as the right hand is concerned, in order to build up speed, keep the second finger strokes as light as possible.

Example 2

We will now add a further two triads to make up a classically sounding chord progression.

Example 3

Although Example 3 is rhythmically different to the previous two examples, the required technique is much the same. The F's in bars two and four should be played with the third finger of the left hand. In order to maintain clarity, these notes should be fretted only when needed, rather than for the duration of the whole measure.

Example 4

The next example uses a similar rhythm to Example 3, but this time the rests have been replaced with pull–offs. This sequence needs to flow smoothly in order to sound effective.

Example 5

Example 5 extends the range of the arpeggio to a third string.

Example 6

Example 6 shows how the arpeggio technique can be of benefit when applied to other aspects of lead playing. Groups of 16th notes are much easier to execute when the first two notes are played using a pull–off. The right-hand technique is the same as that of Example 5 for most of the phrase.

Example 7

Example 7 is similar in style to Example 6.

Example 8

The next example demonstrates how the technique works equally well when applied to triplet rhythms.

Example 9

The final example also consists of triplets. Practice this carefully with a metronome to ensure that the left-hand stretches do not affect the rhythmical accuracy.

Hybrid Picking Chords

DVD VIDEO · Track 4

Of all the styles covered in this book, the hybrid technique is probably most suited to picking out the individual notes of a chord. The main advantage of using Hybrid Picking over standard fingerstyle is to add clarity and definition to the bass notes, as the majority will be played with the pick. The first examples should be used to gain familiarity and a general feel for the technique and make ideal warm–up exercises.

Example 1

Example 1 uses the notes of a C Major chord. It is better to move the right hand slightly from the wrist in a gentle down–up motion rather than making the fingers do all the work. This is the case for all of the examples in this chapter.

Example 2

Example 2 follows the same pattern as Example 1. Whenever the bass note of a chord needs to be played first, it is good practice to fret that note before the others. The chord changes will sound smoother as a result.

Example 3

Example 3 introduces double–stopped notes (two notes played simultaneously).

Example 4

Try and make the next example as "punchy" as possible. The staccato effect is achieved by releasing the left hand pressure immediately after a note has been played.

Example 5

Example 5 uses the same rhythm as Example 4. This time we will alternate the bass note between the root and the fifth.

Example 6

The next example is in three/four time with an ascending bass link at the end of each phrase.

Example 7

Example 7 consists entirely of barre chords. The alternating bass notes are still used.

Example 8

The final example combines all the elements of this chapter. The alternating bass pattern is palm muted throughout.

CHAPTER 5

Using Alternating Pick Strokes

DVD VIDEO | Track 5

The majority of the examples in this chapter serve primarily as exercises aimed at developing the use of alternating pick strokes within Hybrid Picking. This technique will enable the lower notes of phrases to be articulated more efficiently, allowing a better sense of continuity. The real benefits will become more apparent in the following chapters.

Example 1

Before attempting this example, bare in mind the following hints on right-hand technique. Always keep the fleshy part of the palm in contact with the bridge without actually palm muting the string. Use the very tip of the pick, thus minimizing the amount of contact with the string. This will allow for faster picking. Pivot from the wrist only.

$\quad\downarrow = 120$

Example 2

Example 2 requires the same technique as Example 1. The movement of the left hand needs to be well coordinated in order to allow all of the notes to be articulated cleanly.

$\quad\downarrow = 132$

Example 3

Example 3 follows the same sequence of notes as Example 2, this time in the Minor key.

♩ = 132

Example 4

The accuracy needed to execute Example 4 can only be achieved with Hybrid Picking. A little more accuracy is required here because of the introduction of a third string.

♩ = 120

Example 5

In Example 5 we can see how effective the same riff becomes when the lower strings are palm muted slightly.

Example 6

Example 6 reverts back to the use of octaves. The notes used in this example create a more melodious phrase.

Example 7

The remaining two examples lead nicely into the next chapter, showing how alternate picking is an integral part of "Chicken Pickin". The open A string in Example 7 serves as a ground bass and is more effective when palm muted. The second finger plays the intricate higher notes.

Example 8

Example 8 is a country blues riff that makes the most of muting the strings. The last beat of the first measure has four muted notes in a row. Be careful not to produce unwanted harmonics.

CHAPTER 6

"Chicken Pickin"

DVD VIDEO — Track 6

Although "Chicken Pickin" has been linked with country music, we should not forget the advantages of its uses in other genres. The term "Chicken Pickin" describes the actual percussive "popping" sound created by finger or pick articulation, which is often helped along by muting strings with the left hand.

Example 1

The first example shows "Chicken Pickin" in its simplest form. The left-hand first finger should touch the string at all times. Pressure should only be applied after the first two muted notes have been played.

Example 2

Example 2 becomes more effective when the grace notes are added to the start of the riff. Be sure that the intonation is good when executing the bends. This example requires a little strength in the left hand to hold the bends.

Example 3

The bends in the first two measures of Example 3 can be difficult to keep in tune. Practice slowly with a metronome as the rhythm is also tricky. Measures three and four shouldn't be too problematical as the technique involved is that of the previous chapter. Make the muted notes as punchy as possible.

Example 4

The descending notes on the third string in the first measure of this example should all be played with the first finger. This leaves the third finger free to mute the fourth string to give the desired effect. The notes that aren't muted should be as short as possible. It is more comfortable to play the slide in the second measure with the little finger.

Example 5

Try to keep the staccato notes as short as possible in this next example. The picking in the second measure will need some slow practice to master. The muted notes at the end of the third measure can all be stopped with the third finger of the left hand. Don't play too close to the fret as this will prevent unwanted harmonics from being produced.

Example 6

It is important to remember that the technique is still the same in this example despite the triplet feel. It is difficult to maintain continuity throughout the final few measures, so again, slow practice is the key.

Example 7

Example 7 is an effective ascending and descending run in the key of E.

$\quad$ = 120

Example 8

Example 8 develops the idea further to give us a slightly more musical riff. The first two measures require exactly the same treatment as Example 7. Measure 3 should be practiced slowly at first, as the third finger is introduced.

$\quad$ = 116

Example 9

Example 9 is by far the most challenging exercise of the chapter. The continuous 16th note movement demands greater stamina. The combination of hammer–ons and pull–offs make it very awkward to maintain a steady tempo throughout. The artificial harmonics in the fourth measure add a little excitement to the phrase, and should all be played with the third finger of the left hand.

♩ = 116

Runs in Consecutive Intervals

DVD
VIDEO
Track 7

The examples in this chapter demonstrate how the hybrid technique is so effective when playing runs in consecutive intervals. This type of riff is widely used in many musical styles.

Example 1

Example 1 is a descending run in 6ths in the key of G major. This riff should be played as plainly as possible, without any accents or staccato.

Example 2

Example 2 uses the same notes as Example 1. This time slight palm muting should be applied. If this is done correctly, the palm of the right hand will be muting from the fourth string down. When playing this riff, "pop" the second string with more force than in the previous example.

Example 3

As with Example 1, play Example 3 as plainly as possible.

Example 4

By using the same techniques as Example 2, a more "punchy" feel can be achieved.

Example 5

Example 5 is a similar type of phrase, this time in the key of A Major. More strings are introduced in this example.

Example 6

Example 6 returns to the key of G Major for this country sounding riff. The phrase makes use of the open string bounce–downs which are common to this key.

CHAPTER 8

Alternatives to "Sweep Picking"

DVD VIDEO Track 8

Sweep picking is the technique of "sweeping" the pick across two or more strings, usually consisting of notes forming an arpeggio. This effect can be taken to a different level with Hybrid Picking.

Example 1

Example 1 shows the basic idea with which all of the remaining examples adhere to. Always ensure that the pick is lifted to a sufficient height after striking the first note, so as not to mute the other strings. Try to make the rhythm as smooth as possible.

Example 2

Example 2 requires exactly the same technique from the right hand. The triplet notes in this instance are muted. This effect is achieved by placing the third finger of the left hand across strings two, three and four.

Example 3

The third example shows how sweeps are an effective way of adding flair to a jazz phrase. Be sure not to rush through the swing feel of this riff.

Example 4

Example 4 pushes the idea further with this jazz–fusion riff. The sweeps in this example ascend through a diminished seventh chord before descending back to the home key of B Minor via a Jazz Minor scale. The fourth finger of the left hand will need to be strong to execute the first measure accurately.

Example 5

Example 5 has its roots firmly in Country music. This riff works well on the bridge pickup. Make full use of the second finger to "pop" the strings in the second measure.

Example 6

Even though there are some very familiar ideas in Example 6, it is advisable to break the passage down into smaller sections. To play the example all the way through requires stamina and concentration, particularly as there are some tricky left-hand fingerings. Note the two reversed sweeps in the fourth measure.

DVD VIDEO Track 9

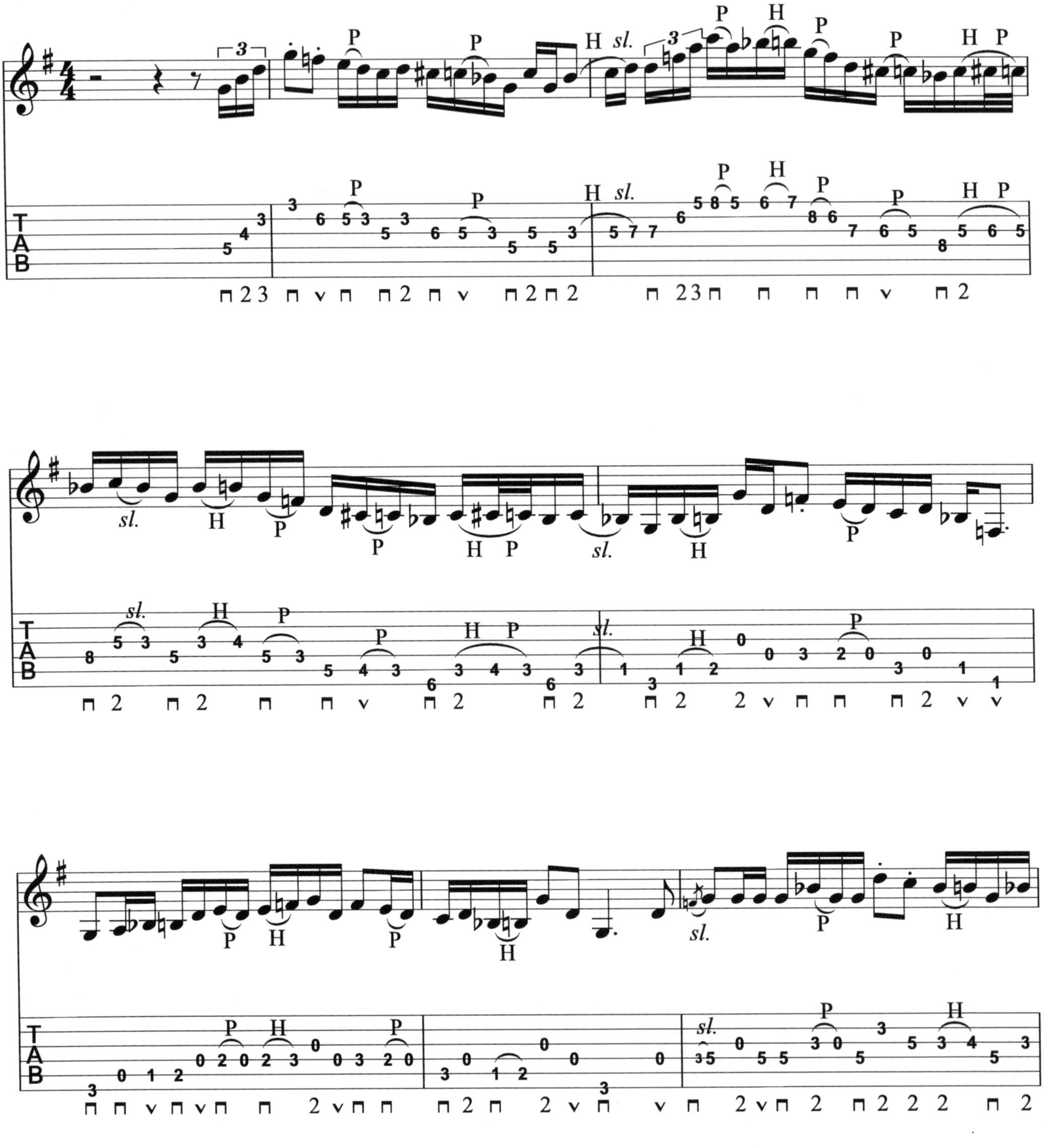

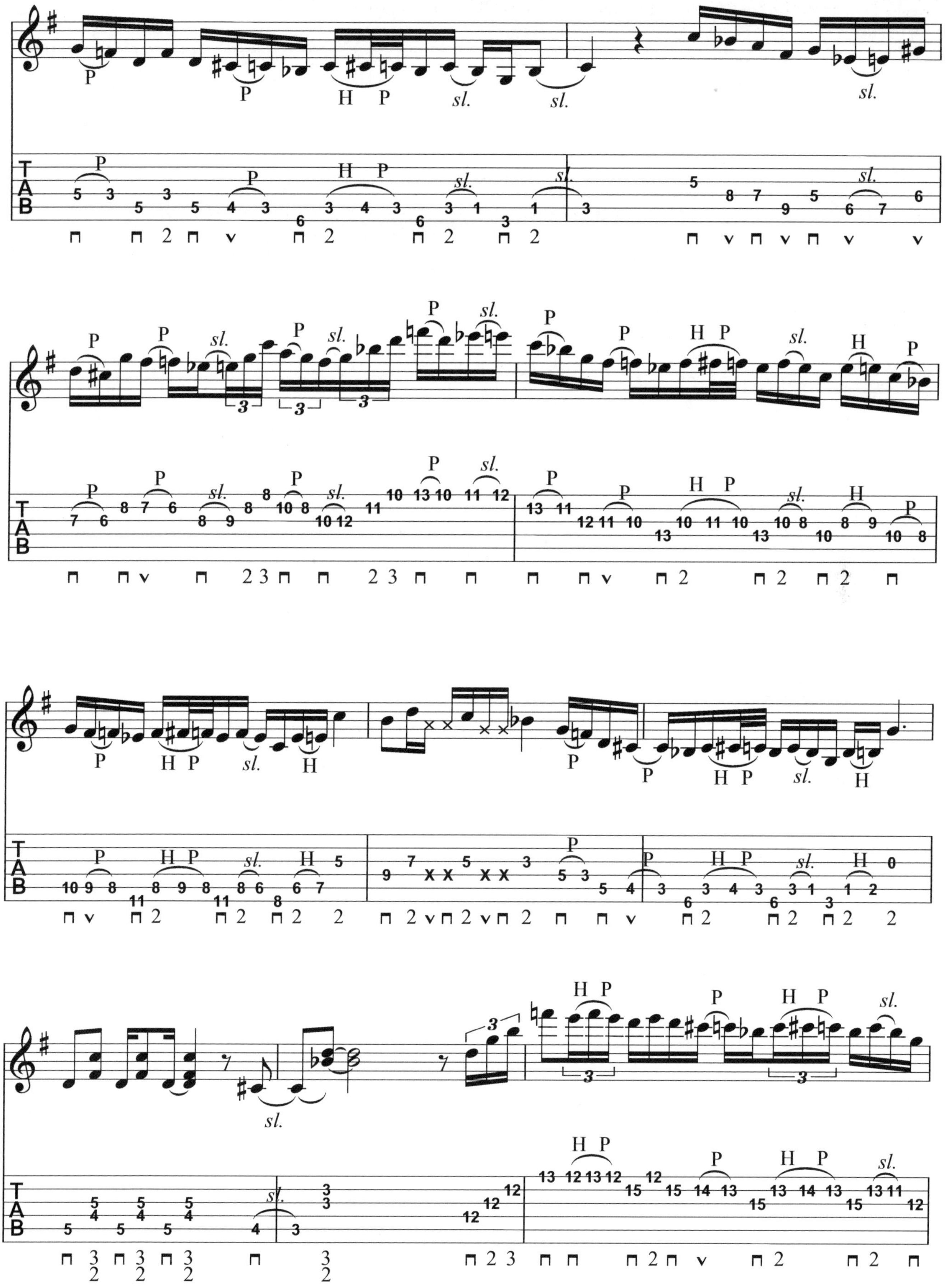

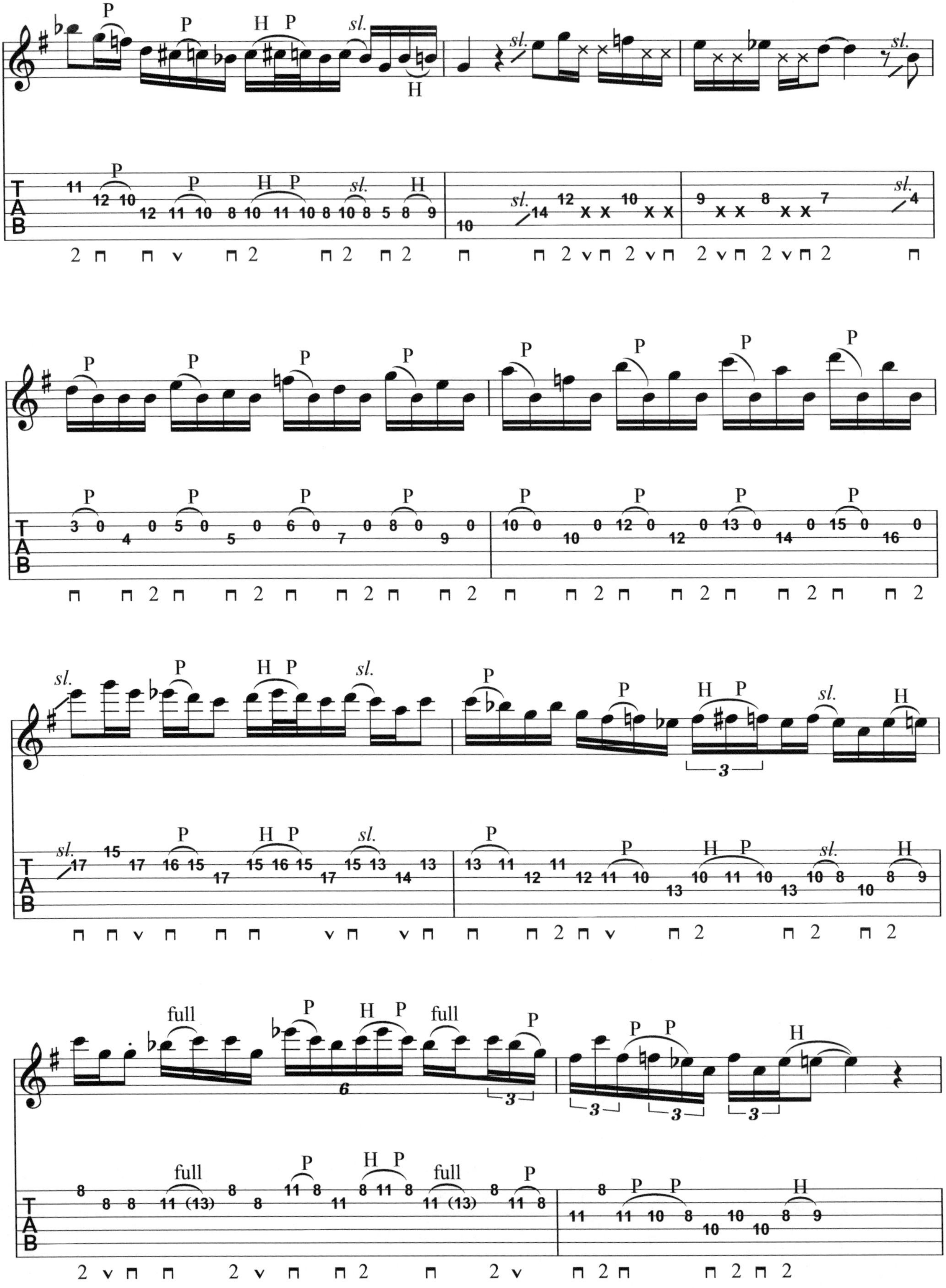
P
H P
sl.
full
T
A
B

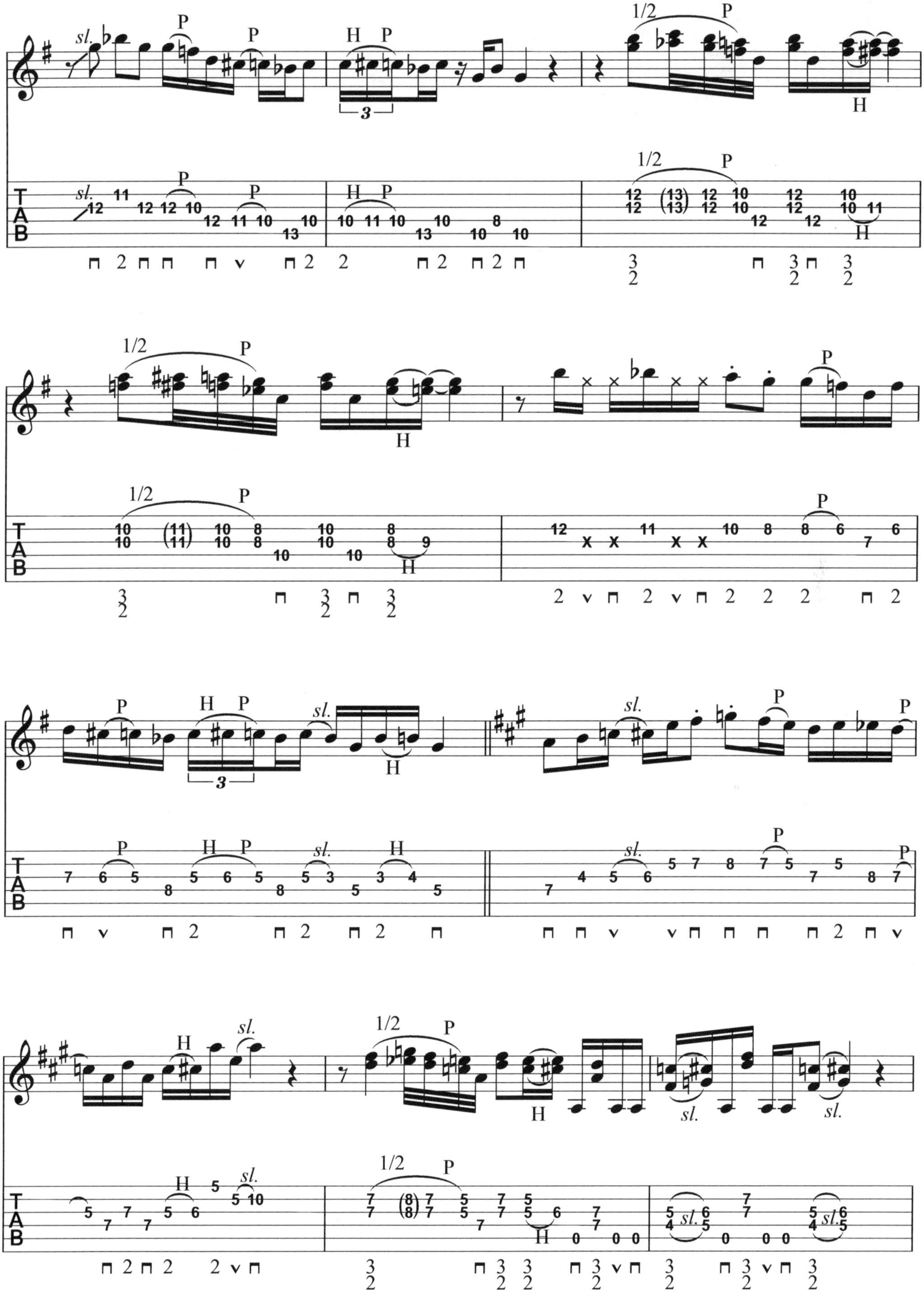

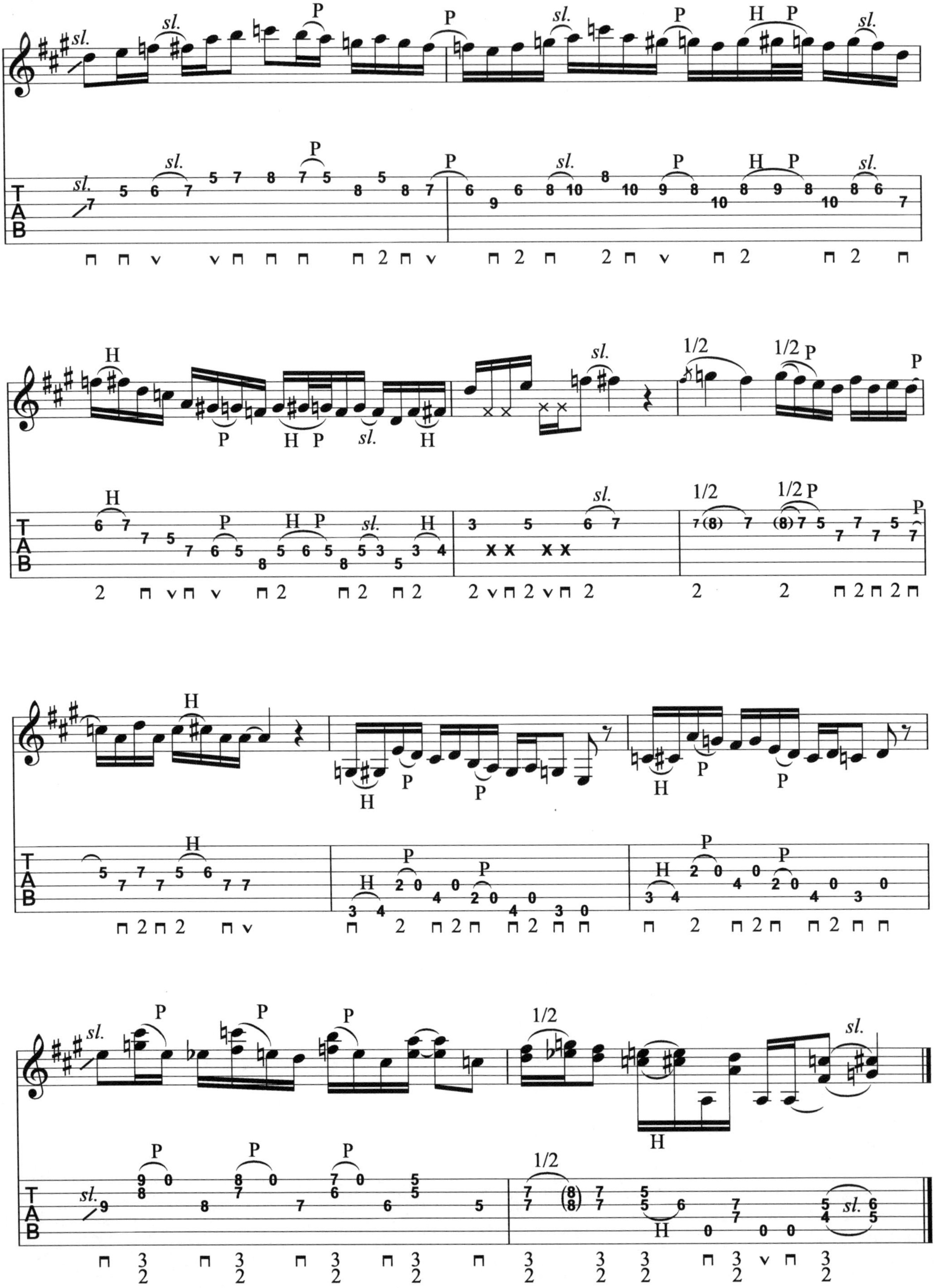

Printed in Great Britain
by Amazon

17127040R00025